THE ENNEA GRAM TEST

Find Who You Are and What You Want in Love, Work, and Relationships in 10 Minutes or Less.

Finding Your Enneagram Type Made Simple!

JOY MAESTRI

© **2018 JOY MAESTRI. All rights reserved.**

The contents of this book may not be reproduced, duplicated or transmitted without direct written permission from the author.

Legal Notice:
You cannot amend, distribute, sell, use, quote or paraphrase any part of the content of this book without the consent of the author.

Disclaimer Notice:
Please note the information contained in this document is for educational and entertainment purposes only. No warranties of any kind are expressed or implied. Readers acknowledge that the author is not engaging in the rendering of legal, financial, medical or professional advice.

By reading this document, the reader agrees that under no circumstances is the author responsible for any losses, direct or indirect, which are incurred as a result of the use of the information contained within this document, including, but not limited to, errors, omissions, or inaccuracies.

TABLE OF CONTENTS

A SPECIAL GIFT

Thank you for purchasing this book! If you have any questions, comments, or concerns throughout the process don't hesitate to shoot an email to gerald@inwardthrive.com. Amazon Best-Selling author Gerald Confienza is a business partner I work with and will readily address any of your concerns.

As a gift, I will send you a print-ready PDF of the Enneagram Test and an exclusive membership to my newsletter *Weekly Enneagram Wisdom*. All you have to do is punch in your name and email here: http://bit.ly/EnneagramGift and send a screenshot of your purchase receipt once prompted. That is all!

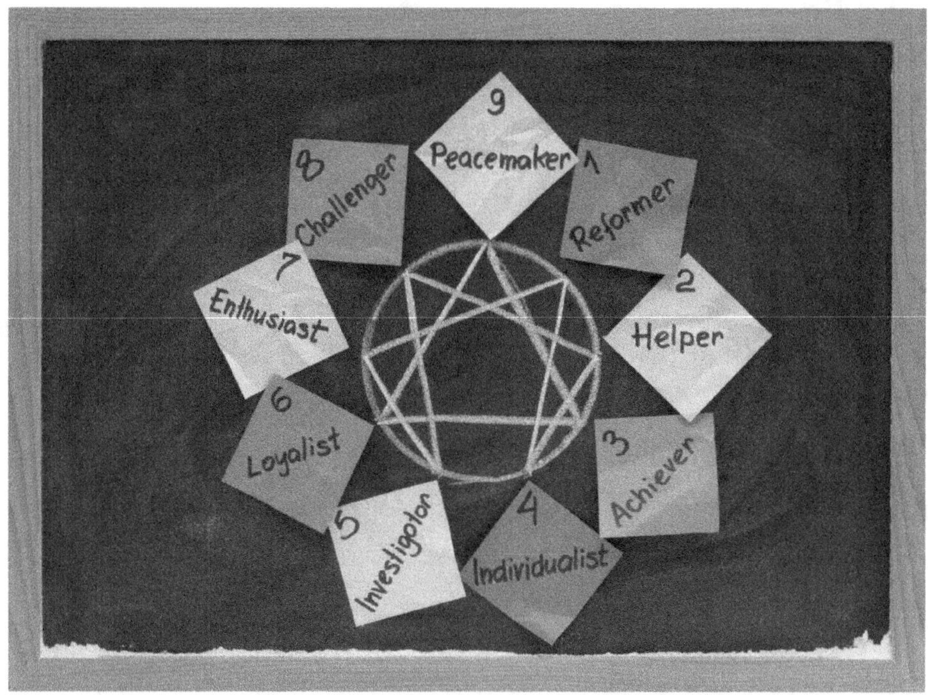

Go to http://bit.ly/EnneagramGift for your FREE gift!

INTRODUCTION TO THE ENNEAGRAM

The Enneagram (*Greek: ennea-gram meaning nine-model*) is a personality typing system based around nine distinct personality types - the theory being that everyone falls into one of these nine categories. Some say that it is an ancient system with its origins traceable to ancient tradition, others suggest that it is much more recent. Ancient system or not, the enneagram is nevertheless effective and more complex than you'd think.

The Enneagram and You

The Enneagram not only focuses on determining the way you cope with reality, but it predicts changes in your personality according to emotional states, namely stress and thriving. Thus, you can get a meta-level awareness of yourself- and the reasons behind your thoughts, words, decisions and actions. Pretty amazing, huh? But! You've got to be ready. You have to be prepared to hear and discover things about yourself that you may not necessarily want to know. As you can see, this can be a tough procedure. We all have an image of who we are and most would rather stick with this image than have their beliefs challenged.

It's recommended that you ask a very close friend to give some feedback if you're unsure of your results after taking the test. Also, don't get hung up about the negative traits of your personality. Instead, pour all your energy into developing the positive aspects of your character.

The Enneagram and Others

Personal awareness is just the start. Using the Enneagram to understand the fluctuation in personality of others is makes it all the more interesting. Careful study of it will make you more sensible to the personality of others, allow for more understanding, and give you a framework through which you can help them cope with the adversities of life.

A Few Points to Bear in Mind

- This is one of many tests you can take that will start you on the path to understanding your Enneagram type. Within the field of Enneagram studies, tests are only suggestions: they indicate a starting point and not a conclusion.

- Understand that all personality types are essentially positive and that any negative behavior you may become aware of in your (or others') type can be remedied.

- Beware of putting people in a box and limiting your personality or that of others to an Enneagram category. *E.g. Someone being a Seven doesn't necessarily mean that they are uncommitted or scattered.*

- Use this knowledge to grow your understanding and appreciation for the fellow humans that accompany us in this path called life.

ENNEAGRAM PERSONALITY TYPES 1 - 9

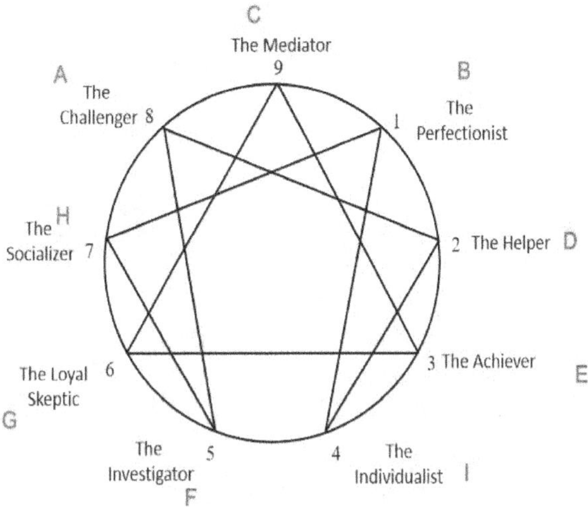

There are 9 personality types, each one communes with one another.

Please use this chapter as reference after having taken the test and figured out your dominant type. Note that the results of this test are not one hundred percent definitive and that there is a degree of error inherent with every psychological test. Therefore, don't consider yourself as "branded", "labeled" or "tagged" with a personality type.

As you read through each of these personality type overviews, you will see yourself, friends or family in them! It's amazing how accurate these type overviews can be. That's the beauty of the Enneagram. Make sure to also read over the *workplace, love, and mental health* descriptions & recommendations below each type overview. Enjoy!

Wings

It's important to note that there is no 'pure' type and that whatever your dominant type is, you also have a 'wing' or second most dominant type. Your second most dominant type is one of the two adjacent types from your position on the Enneagram. E.g. If you're type 1, then your wing is either 9 or 2. Likewise, if you're a type 3, then your wing is either a 2 or a 4. It's your job to identify what wing you lean most towards.

Centers

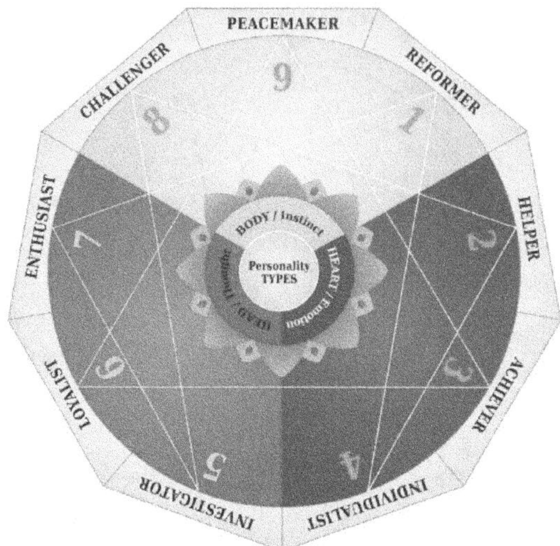

The Enneagram above is divided into three centers: The Body, Heart, and Head Centers.
It is believed that our ego-identification and sense of identity derives from an emotional
response to a lack of unity consciousness.

- For types 8, 9, and 1 occupying the Body (Instinct) center, their emotion is *anger* and the
  adopting of their identity is the way they cope with it. Though Nines and Ones don't
  tend to express physical anger, it's because they don't give themselves permission to. Out
  of the three types in the Body center, only Eights (The Challenger) allow themselves to
  show their anger.

- For types 2, 3, and 4 occupying the Heart (Feeling) center, their emotion is *shame*. To
  overcome their sense of shame, Twos seek approval, Threes strive to become valuable,
  and Fours try to be unique.

- For types 5, 6, and 7 occupying the Head (Thinking) center, their emotion is *fear*. To
  overcome their fear, Fives try to become capable, Sixes seek protection in something
  greater than themselves, and Sevens keep themselves engaged and entertained.

Levels of Development

As a human matures spiritually and is less identified by his or her ego, they can transcend personality types, develop understanding and compassion for all types, and can adopt the healthy traits of each. That's what we'll refer to a *healthy* type. The opposite is also true. The more we grow in ego-identification (the *unhealthier* we are), the more we adopt the negative traits of our type. As our mental health further deteriorates, these lower qualities begin to deteriorate our lives.

Type 1: Reformer

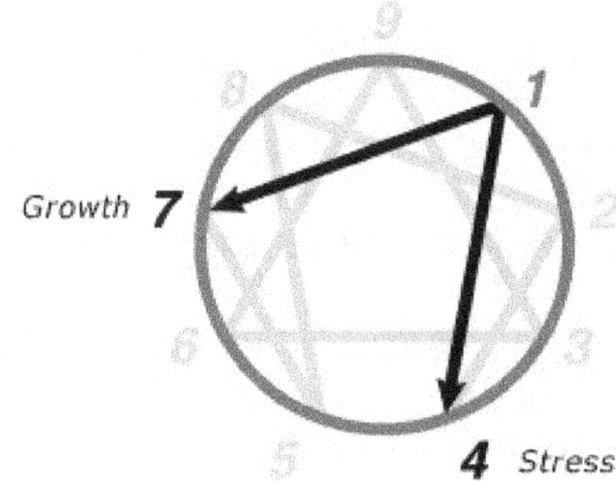

Taken from enneagraminstitute.com

General Overview:

Reformers are inclined to change and innovation. They like to improve things and leave them better than how they found them. They are generally impatient and perfectionists with the things they do. Their main purpose in most situations is to get things done and they usually assume a leadership role. They are often independent and very competitive. They have a tendency to prioritize work even when it may prevent them from experiencing pleasurable activities.

Wing can be either 9 or 2.

Fears being evil or corrupted.

Longs to be good and have integrity.

Under stress, 1s will behave like an average or unhealthy 4.

As they grow, 1s will adopt healthy qualities of a 7.

In Love:

Uncommonly mature and independent, Ones will bring about strong ethical standards, the desire to serve others, values and practical perspectives to the relationship.

They are occasionally reserved, especially at first, as they're the type that isn't likely to show all of their feelings. However, they are willing to commit to a relationship and provide security for their partner in this sense. Their strong sense of purpose can be very attractive for their partner and usually secures Ones with important positions in organizations.

Areas for Improvement: Their stiff nature doesn't permit them to express their feelings adequately. Thus, if they are dissatisfied in a relationship, they tend not to openly admit it. Their idealism could become overbearing, arouse irritability, and have them become too critical of their partner.

In the Workplace:

Reformers are usually best suited for creative positions such as those found in research and development, strategic planning, and product design. They pay attention to every detail of a project in a way that contributes to its overall performance. They tend to have uneasy relationships with their co-workers as they demand a lot from them. However, they can also assume the role of mentors to those who are interested in learning from an experienced figure. They don't rest until the job is done and can be considered as workaholics.

Mental health:

Reformers tend to have a low level of tolerance towards mistakes. They usually find it hard to be relaxed since they are always thinking about fulfilling a goal. Because of this, they are prone to getting stressed and it may complicate their relationships with those around them. They rarely communicate how they feel, which may result in later emotional problems. Responsibility is of great importance in the reformers' lives. Since they are hardworking and get the job done, they often feel fulfilled and satisfied when completing a task. They find meaning in doing things.

Notable 1s: St. Augustine, Martin Luther, Julie Andrews, Hanan Ashrawi, Noam Chomsky, John Cleese, Hillary Clinton, Confucius, Anderson Cooper, Ann Coulter, Jane Curtin, Anne Frank, Harrison Ford, Jodie Foster, John Fund, Buckminster Fuller, Melinda Gates, Emma Goldman, Barry Goldwater, Amy Goodman, Al Gore, Stephen Jay Gould, The Puritans (general), The Amish (general), Eleanor Roosevelt, George Bernard Shaw, Martha Stewart, Harry Truman, Carl Sagan.

Type 2: The Helper

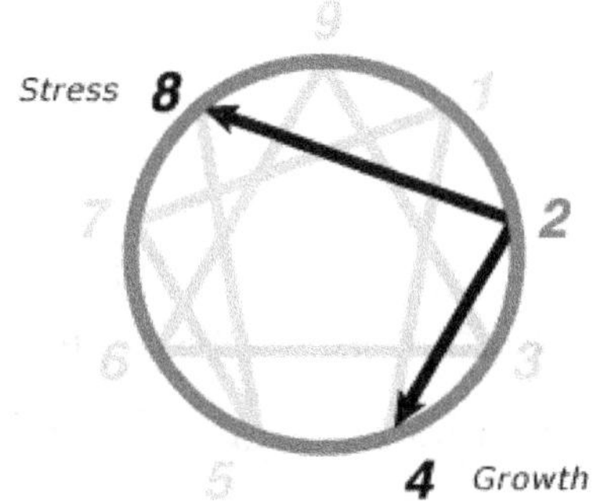

Taken from enneagraminstitute.com

General Overview:

Helpers are empathic, warm and friendly people. They care for those around them and go out of their way to help those in need. They are nurturing, altruistic and sincere towards others. They have no problem being generous and giving more than they should. Personal relationships are of the highest value for them. They often have problems acknowledging their own needs and their perceived self-worth relies on being needed by others. Therefore, they often lend a helping hand in order to be perceived as saviors. This is their path to influence and power.

Wing can be either 1 or 3.

Fears being unlovable.

Longs to be needed and loved.

Under stress, 2s may behave like an unhealthy 8.

As they grow, 2s will adopt healthy qualities of a 4.

In Love:

Similar to Ones, Twos are also unusually mature and independent in their relationships, as get their emotional needs from their altruistic endeavors. Twos usually help their partners soften, relax and feel at ease with them, which is something that types like Ones, Threes, and Eights really need. Twos are steady, reliable, and truthful.

Areas for Improvement: Though Twos don't care much about receiving public appreciation, however, they do expect to be appreciated in private by their partner. In an unhealthy state, if Twos feel unappreciated, they may become smothering and manipulative. Because their type is outward-dependent, introspection and self-understanding are things Twos could improve on.

In the workplace:

They are best suited for helping professions such as psychologists, nurses, teachers and social workers. They like to have a good relationship with their co-workers and don't mind doing some of their work in order to please them and tend to avoid competition with them. They usually value their work relationships more than the financial or material benefits obtained from the job.

Mental health:

Helpers depend on their relationships with others. Being altruistic and needed makes them feel fulfilled. A failure to being recognized as a caring person may result in bitterness, resentment, even aggression. They may forget about their priorities in order to satisfy the needs or demands of others. As long as Helpers feel their help is appreciated, they can be at peace with themselves and with the rest of the world.

Notables 2s: Jesus, Diana-Princess of Wales, Mother Theresa, Bill Cosby, Celine Dion, Mr. Rogers, Farrah Fawcett, Melissa Gilbert, Danny Glover, Whitney Houston, Arianna Huffington, Laura Huxley, Andrea Jaeger, Craig Kielburger, Madonna, Alma Mahler, Imelda Marcos, Mira Milosovic, Florence Nightingale, Merlin Olsen, Christina Onassis, Yoko Ono, Suze Orman, Priscilla Presley, Rev. Robert Schuller, Richard Simmons, Danielle Steel, Sally Struthers, Actor Richard Thomas, Ivana Trump, Desmond Tutu.

Type 3: The Achiever

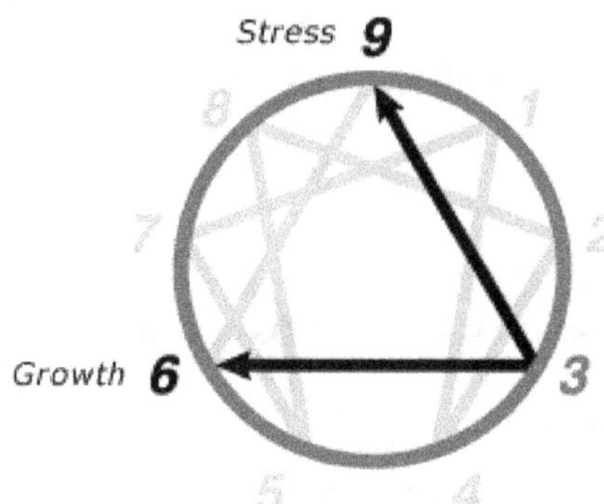

Taken from enneagraminstitute.com

General Overview:

Achievers are competitive and result oriented. They are ambitious when pursuing a goal, they place success at the top of their needs and avoid being perceived as losers at all costs. The most important thing for an Achiever is to be recognized as a competent person that gets what they want. They are confident, socially competent, good networkers and charismatic. They use those skills to make their plans come true and don't care if someone gets hurt in the process.

Wing can be either 2 or 4.

Fears being worthless.

Longs to feel valuable.

Under stress, 3s may behave like an unhealthy 9.

As they grow, 3s will adopt healthy qualities of a 6.

In Love:

Because Threes can be dazzling, high energy, impressive for their accomplishments, their partner usually feels admiration for them. This is what Threes secretly strive for- being someone even their lover can admire. That's why Threes do well with types that would rather have the spotlight on others instead of themselves. Oh, and they don't really do drama. Instead, Threes are proactive people who will nurture and coach their partners into the pursuit of their goals. In a healthy relationship, Threes will have a vision for the relationship and proactive work to make it a reality.

Area for Improvement: Trouble with time commitments, lack of emotional attachment, and even (depending on your type) competition are things that Threes struggle with consistently. Additionally, Threes are normally unaware of their feelings, and even if they take notice of them, they tend not to verbalize them. They can become easily critical of others if they don't measure up to their expectations- that includes their partner.

In the workplace:

They are highly competitive and tend to ascend quickly through the ranks of an organization. They plan their strategies with the purpose of serving their own needs. They are generally good negotiators and tend to make no concessions. They are better suited for positions that require cold-blooded decisions to be taken.

Mental health:

Achievers often focus too much on the popular conception of success. Therefore, they may fail to recognize what they truly want and need. Because they put success before anything else, their personal relationships are prone to be full of conflict and may not last too long. Since they almost always achieve what they want to do, they experience a great deal of satisfaction and feel fulfilled as doers.

Notable 3s: Arnold Schwarzenegger, Michael Jordan, Mick Jagger, Elvis Presley, Anthony Robbins, Muhammad Ali, Lance Armstrong, David Bowie, Les Brown, Jack Canfield, Courtney Cox, Tom Cruise, Michael Dell, F. Scott Fitzgerald, Diane Sawyer, O.J. Simpson, Duchess of Windsor Wallis Simpson, Will Smith, Sylvester Stallone, Sting, Sharon Stone, Raquel Welch, Vanessa Williams, Marianne Williamson, Oprah Winfrey, Natalie Wood, Tiger Woods.

Type 4: The Individualist

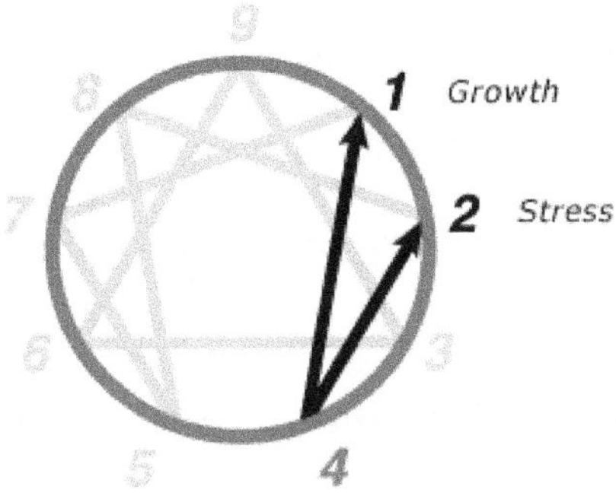

Taken from enneagraminstitute.com

General Overview:

Individualists are inclined to self-determination, uniqueness, and self-expression. They tend to like art and things that make them feel different from the rest. They want, above all, to be perceived as special, interesting, and superior. They want to be set apart from the common people and resent to be considered average. Because of this, they sometimes feel separated from others and fail to enjoy shared pleasurable activities. They are often introspective, romantic and sensitive. They often experience feelings of vulnerability, melancholy, and loneliness caused by the distance between them and those around. They are prone to fantasizing and imagining themselves as the most important being in existence.

Wing can be either 3 or 5.

Fears not knowing who they are.

Longs find a sense of identity.

Under stress, 4s will behave like an average or unhealthy 2.

As they grow, 4s will adopt healthy qualities of a 1.

In Love:

Fours make for great lovers. They bring about creativity, intense emotions, sexual freedom, mystery, unmatched humor, dreams and other magical elements into the relationship like no other type. They love details and subtlety and will find creative ways to express their love. Because they want their world to be beautiful, they strive to maintain an elegant and aesthetic frame while helping you do the same. Be sure to express your gratitude, Fours love feeling appreciated for their uniqueness.

Areas for Improvement: Fours' idealism and perfectionism may be too much for their partner to bear. In short, they can be elitist snobs who become condescending to those whose refinement is not up to par. In an unhealthy state, Fours can be unforgiving, hopelessly emotional, passive-aggressive, self-indulgent, and attention-seeking. They're naturally slow to trust. So, when conflict emerges, trust can go out the window for all he or she cares. Periods of 'testing' that may follow can get intense.

In the workplace:

Individualists have a hard time working in groups as they feel they won't get the same attention as if they were working alone. They like to be recognized for their achievements and often take credit for the work of others. Their main motivation is to advance their careers, which in their minds is more important than the success of the group or the organization.

Mental health:

Individualists tend to experience feelings of isolation due to their desire of being set apart from the rest. They find pleasure in being unique and special, but at the same time, they risk falling into depression due to a feeling of detachment towards those who surround them. They are self-absorbed and often feel misunderstood, which in turn drives their desire of rising above the rest to perceive themselves as valuable. They often struggle to balance their need for protagonism with their need for intimacy.

Notable 4s: Vincent Van Gogh, Michael Jackson, Morrissey, Edgar Allen Poe, Bjork, Kate Bush, Nicolas Cage, Prince Charles, Mary Higgins Clark, Eric Clapton, Kurt Cobain, Paula Cole, Judy Collins, Cheryl Crow, Neil Diamond, Bob Dylan, Judy Garland, Martha Graham, Jewel, Angelina Jolie, Janis Joplin, Marilyn Manson, Frank McCourt, Petrarch, Pink Floyd (in general), Sylvia Plath, Alan Watts, Orson Welles.

Type 5: The Investigator

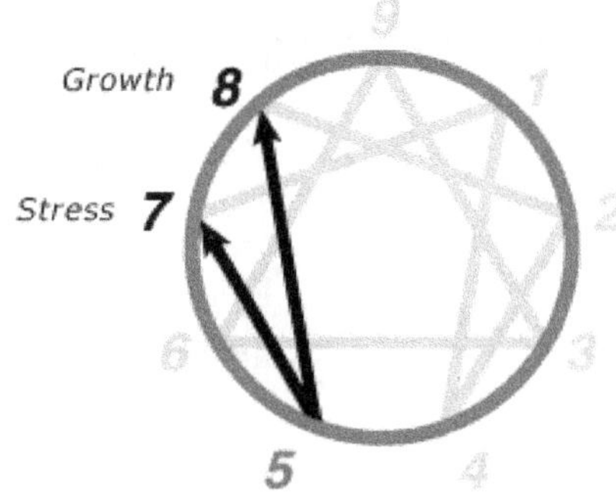

Taken from enneagraminstitute.com

General Overview:

Investigators are oriented towards complex ideas, innovation, and thought-provoking themes. They are curious, inventive and tend to be visionaries. They prefer activities that require intellectual effort and enjoy thinking about abstract concepts. They are interested in art, philosophy, and science. They may be shy and tend to isolate themselves and withdraw from social life. They are sometimes preoccupied with their thoughts and worry about not fitting in. They are arrogant sometimes and distance themselves from others. Freedom is one of the most important things in life for them.

Wing can be either 4 or 6.

Fears feeling incapable.

Longs to achieve mastery or feel capable.

Under stress, 5s will behave like an average or unhealthy 7.

As they grow, 5s will adopt qualities of an 8.

In Love:

Definitely not the basic type. Fives in love are objective but profound, mentally stimulating, and sexually adventurous. Though they won't show it, Fives secretly love attention and affection and will treasure those who provide this. Because of their reduced social circles, they actively protect and nourish the few people they have let into their lives and thus enjoy very deep connections with them. Fives are devoted to their craft, remain calm under crisis, are great decision-makers, and easily the best listeners out of all the other types (their undivided attention is yours!).

Areas for improvement: Fives love debate and rational back-and-forths. This can be an attractive trait for, say, Twos, but can be a turn off for other types. Fives often develop cold and even nihilistic life perspectives, coming to the conclusion that there's no point in anything. It's no surprise then that in unhealthy relationships, Fives may become self-contained, idle, and isolated- only engaging with their partners when they 100% have to. Fives are very wary of their personal space and will resent those who intrude upon it.

In the workplace:

They are best suited for tasks that demand creativity and investigative skills, such as scientific research, forensic analyses, and the arts. They like to create effective solutions to existing problems, analyze the different possible options to face a challenge, and use state of the art methods to improve processes. They are not very sociable towards their co-workers and prefer to work alone most of the time.

Mental health:

Investigators tend to withdraw from social life because they are generally more interested in things than in people. This withdrawal is not always unhealthy, although sometimes it might bring negative consequences such as feelings of loneliness and lack of belonging. However, some of them might isolate themselves without feeling uncomfortable, because they might find solitary activities like reading more enjoyable than social activities such as going to parties.

Notable 5s: Siddartha Gautama (The Buddha), St. Thomas Aquinas, Albert Einstein, Issac Asimov, Osama bin Laden, Tim Burton, Marie Curie, Daniel Day-Lewis, Charles Darwin, René Descartes, Albert Einstein, T. S. Eliot, Bill Gates, J. Paul Getty, Stephen Hawking, Alfred Hitchcock, Franz Kafka, Jacqueline Kennedy Onassis, J. Robert Oppenheimer, Al Pacino, Jean-Paul Sartre, Nikola Tesla, Neil Young.

Type 6: The Loyalist

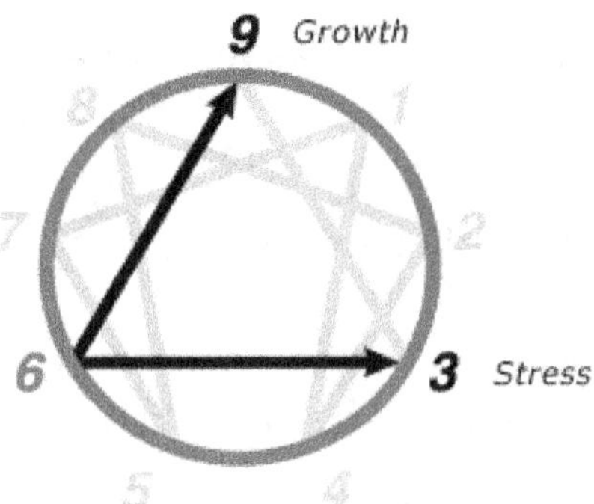

Taken from enneagraminstitute.com

General Overview:

Loyalists are reliable, hardworking and trustworthy people. They take responsibility and protect their close ones, even if it may carry negative consequences. They are security-oriented and always think about what might go wrong in diverse situations. That's why they foresee and solve problems that others might not be able to. They may have trust issues and doubt about those they care about and themselves. Although they might be suspicious of most people, they become loyal once they feel trust can be given. Above all, they adhere religiously to systems, beliefs, or groups of people because they bring about a sense of security for Sixes. However, that can also be because they don't trust their inner guidance and look for it elsewhere.

Wing can be either 5 or 7.

Fears not having support.

Longs to find support and security.

Under stress, 6s will adopt unhealthy qualities of a 3.

As they grow, 6s will adopt healthy qualities of a 9.

In Love:

Sixes and relationships? Well, sixes are loyal (yup, you guessed it!), warm, generous, playful and connect with their partner in a very profound way. The grounding energy that characterize healthy Sixes will prove to be irresistible for the likes of a Two or Three and are the reason why Sixes make for great long-term partners. Though insecure at first, once having established a bond with their partner, a Six will exude commitment, strength, devotion, and unquestioned loyalty.

Areas for improvement: Because of their adherence to systems, beliefs, or social groups, Sixes will spend a lot of time on, say, their job and may disregard other aspects of their life. Likewise, Sixes will think twice before saying or doing anything that may change the status quo of the relationship they're in. Change means uncertainty and that's the last thing Sixes want. Because of this, Sixes may harbor pent-up emotions. Unhealthy Sixes in a state of uncertainty may become scattered, reactive, and suspicious with feelings of inferiority and will desperately seek out stronger authorities or beliefs that will ground them in place again.

In the workplace:

Loyalists do well in security-related tasks such as public security planning, industrial security, people protection and law enforcement. They often assume the role of protectors towards those around them. They foresee the problems an organization might face and are always thinking about the risks of making a certain decision. They tend to identify themselves with the organization they work with and prefer long-term jobs to short-term ones.

Mental health:

They often have problems getting close to other people and very frequently have trust issues. That's why they are extremely loyal to those they think they can trust, as they feel loved ones in their lives are scarce. They tend to fear many things even when there is little or no reason to feel that way. That's why they are always focused on security and preventing anything that may go wrong.

Famous 6s: Sigmund Freud, Malcolm X, Mark Twain, Woody Allen, George H. W. Bush, John Cusack, Rodney Dangerfield, Larry David, Ellen DeGeneres, Mel Gibson, Ed Harris, Adolf Hitler, J. Krishnamurti, Richard Nixon, Chuck Norris, Julia Roberts, Pat Robertson, Steven Seagal, Bruce Springsteen, Jon Stewart, Ben Stiller, Patrick Swayze, Shirley Temple, Uma Thurman, Meg Tilly, Linda Tripp, Bono.

Type 7: The Enthusiast

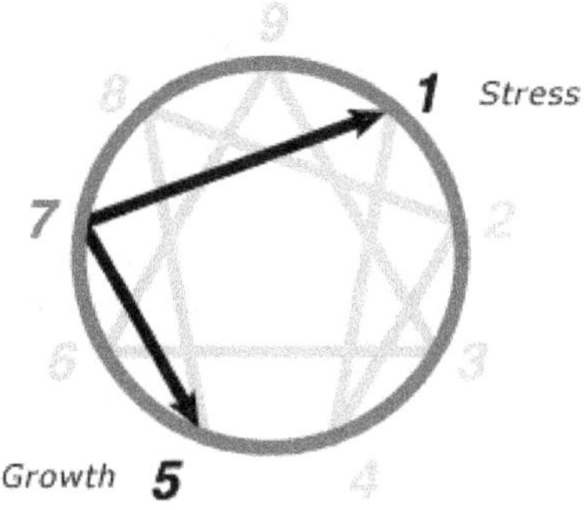

Taken from enneagraminstitute.com

General Overview:

Enthusiasts are spontaneous, optimistic and full of energy. They like to connect with other people and are good networkers. They are constantly seeking new exciting experiences and distractions. They make a lot of plans and are future-oriented, always wondered what might happen next. They are open-minded to new ideas and other cultures and systems of belief. They sometimes lack discipline and may fail to complete the tasks they set themselves. They cope with negative feelings by looking for distractions that help them forget about bad experiences.

Wing can be either 6 or 8.

Fears not having joy in their life.

Longs to be happy and content

Under stress, 7s will behave like an unhealthy 1.

As they grow, 7s will adopt healthy qualities of a 5.

In Love:

Funny, high-energy, outgoing people with a brilliant mind ready to plunge ahead, see possibilities, and inspire others. Sevens will get their partner seeing the positive in everything, nothing can go wrong in their daily pursuits. They can be great complements to stiff and harsh Threes or Eights and cool and unassuming Fives. Their romantic and adventurous side will have them providing their partner with exquisite experiences, even if it means 'slightly' overspending! Usually being the life of the party, Sevens can turn their experiences or catastrophes into amazing stories that will light up the spirits in any social setting (despite their partner's moodiness).

Areas for Improvement: They're terrible at managing the painful or negative aspects of anything, including their relationships. Under stress, they're likely to direct their emotions to someone or something, instead of owning up to them. Their quick tongue that would've otherwise been their charm, is now likely to get them in trouble as they may be quick to insult. Under contempt, Sevens are very strong-willed and will avoid feeling controlled or manipulated. In unhealthy states, Sevens will be the cause behind public scenes or reckless behavior that others would cringe at.

In the workplace:

They are better suited for non-repetitive and entertainment related tasks such as vacation-planning, tourism, and artistic activities. Enthusiasts present themselves in a warm and friendly way. They motivate co-workers to take action and fill the organization with motivation. They like to plan even though they may not always carry out their plan because they might get distracted by other tasks.

Mental health:

Enthusiasts emotional stability depends on always having the chance to do something they like. They can't stand boredom and idleness and love to feel pleasure above anything else. They don't like to worry about things, which in turn may cause that their problems get bigger as they are not taken care of. They are prone to addictions, be it food, drugs, or experiences. Therefore, they must be very careful with the consequences of their behaviors.

Famous of 7s: Leonardo DaVinci, Steve Jobs, Winston Churchill, Britney Spears, Steve Wozniak, Tim Allen, Jeff Bezos, Jacqueline Bisset, Richard Branson, Mel Brooks, Casanova, Jackie Chan, George Clooney, Katie Couric, Stephen Covey, Gérard Depardieu, Cameron Diaz, Leonardo DiCaprio, Angie Dickinson, Robert Downey, Thomas Jefferson, Elton John, John F. Kennedy, Brad Pitt, Steven Spielberg, Barbra Streisand, Tina Turner.

Type 8: The Challenger

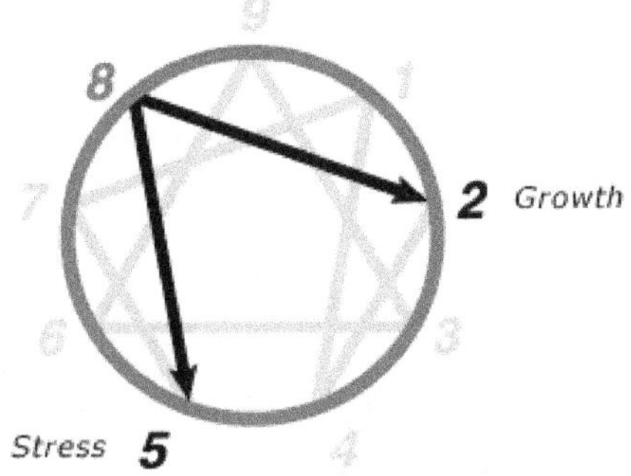

Taken from enneagraminstitute.com

General Overview:

Challengers are assertive, self-confident and sometimes aggressive. They are dominant towards others and decisive when taking action. They don't beat around the bush and are straight talkers about anything. Confrontation is a behavior they often engage into, as they like to impose themselves over others. Although they might be perceived as unfriendly sometimes, they are considered leaders and doers. They don't tolerate failure from others and don't like to be vulnerable. That's why they are not very open-minded and their trust is very hard to gain.

Wing can be either 7 or 9.

Fears being vulnerable or harmed.

Longs to have control and be capable of self-protection

Under stress, 8s will behave like an unhealthy 5.

As they grow, 8s will adopt healthy qualities of a 2.

In Love:

Eights are bound to bring an inspiring vision and sense of purpose to the relationship. They're willing to make sacrifices to make this vision a reality. Usually the dominant ones in a relationship, Eights are exciting, physical and very passionate, traits many types will find sexy. They're the kind that wants their partner to feel proud of them and want to have around them people who will recognize their leadership, energy, and (even) brashness. Their dominance provides a sense of security and grounding for their partner. They can be very reliable.

Areas for Improvement: Eights protect their sense of purpose and will feel repulsed from their partner if they attempt taking that away from them. On the negative end of the spectrum, Eights are bossy, controlling and selfish. They want the last word in every argument. Relationships with Eights can end up in a power play to see who's the dominant one. Unhealthy Eights may become physically and verbally violent, instigating their partner to leave them because of fear.

In the workplace:

They are better suited for positions of leadership such as management, project development, and public relations. They like to get things done even if it means a deterioration of their work relations. They don't tolerate lazy or weak co-workers. They want the organization to be strong and don't mind taking charge of difficult situations and present solutions. They are highly motivated to ascend to the higher ranks of an organization and don't feel guilty if it affects their co-workers negatively.7

Mental health:

Challengers tend to be aggressive, temperamental and sometimes prone to violence. They want things to be done their way and don't tolerate weakness. They avoid being vulnerable and are closed towards the affection of others. Their trust isn't gained easily but once they feel comfortable with someone they stand by them. They don't tolerate betrayal under any circumstances.

Famous 8s: Napoleon Bonaparte, Fidel Castro, Morgan Freeman, Saddam Hussein, Mao Tse-tung, Rosie O'Donnell, Shaquille O'Neal, Bill O'Reilly, Julia Phillips, Iggy Pop, Queen Latifah, Theodore Roosevelt, Axl Rose, Tupac Shakur, Ariel Sharon, Gene Simmons, Frank Sinatra, Donald Trump, Denzel Washington, Keenan Ivory Wayans.

Type 9: The Peacemaker

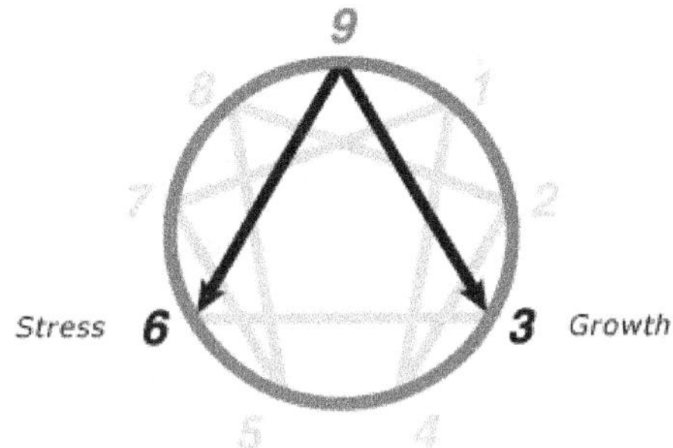

Taken from enneagraminstitute.com

General Overview:

Peacemakers are calm, tolerant, and optimistic people. They appreciate calmness and avoid conflict at all costs. But if a conflict does ensue, they do everything they can to resolve it. They prefer things to go smoothly and don't like confrontation. They may even avoid certain experiences or give in to others desires to avoid a discussion. They want to be accepted by others and hope that everything turns out good for everyone. They don't like having enemies and avoid getting upset whenever they can.

Wing can be either 8 or 1.

Fears separation.

Longs to find peace of mind.

Under stress, 9s will behave like an average or unhealthy 6.

As they grow, 9s will adopt qualities of a 3.

In Love:

Willing to put others before themselves, Nines have an alluring soothing effect on their partners. Their gentle, nurturing qualities make it so that most types feel at ease with Nines and feel like they can finally be themselves around them. At last, they have found a place in which they are accepted for who they are, and this is in the arms of a Nine. This is the sensuality of a Nine, the kind that makes their partners abandon their stiff attachment to their ego and find peace. Nines value solidarity, mutual understanding, and the ability to move on, forgive and forget.

Areas for Improvement: When things start getting bad, Nines withdraw from the relationship. It's like they're not there, and it makes their partners go crazy. Nines begin to tune out, become unable to speak of what troubles them, and their stubbornness surfaces. Unhealthy Nines are unable to own up to their responsibilities, engage in massive passive-aggressive behavior, and, if they do speak up, will blame their partner for repressed feelings that they may have been carrying along for years. As relationships with Nines worsen, they begin to drift apart and are unlikely to be the first to apologize.

In the workplace:

They are better suited for tasks such as conflict-solving, human resource management, and social work. They tend to avoid competition with co-workers in order to prevent confrontation and conflict. Therefore, they may miss on opportunities to be recognized as a valuable part of the organization or to obtain a promotion. Calmness in the workplace is the most important thing for a peacemaker.

Mental health:

Pacemakers value stability and tranquility above anything else. They avoid confrontation even if it means preventing them from obtaining benefits. Therefore, they get very stressed when dealing with conflicting situations and do anything in their power to end a discussion quickly and effectively. Their emotional stability depends on a lack of aggressiveness in their lives.

Famous 9s: The Dalai Lama, Mahatma Gandhi, Jennifer Aniston, David Beckham, Sandra Bullock, Bill Clinton, Actor Jeff Daniels, Dwight Eisenhower, Queen Elizabeth II, Will Ferrell, Mahatma Gandhi, Abraham Lincoln, Ronald Reagan, Gena Rowlands, Rita Rudner, Ringo Starr, Gloria Steinem, Daniel Stern, James Stewart, Actor Eric Stoltz, Studs Terkel, Billy Bob Thornton, Jack Warden.

THE ENNEAGRAM TEST

Instructions

Please read these instructions carefully before starting the test. This test is designed to assess your personality type according to the Enneagram of Personality theory. Mark all your answers on the answer sheet and write only where indicated. DO NOT write on this booklet.

In the provided answer sheet, write your name, gender, age, and the date in which you are taking the test. This questionnaire contains 126 statements. Please read carefully each one of them and mark with a circle the answer you believe is the better description of how you stand on each statement.

Mark "SD" if the statement is completely false or if you **strongly disagree** with it.

(SD)····DI····N····AG····SA

Mark "DI" if the statement is almost completely false or if you **disagree** with it.

SD····(DI)····N····AG····SA

Mark "N" if the statement is almost equally false or true, if you can't decide, or if you are **neutral** towards the statement.

SD····DI····(N)····AG····SA

Mark "AG" if the statement is almost completely true or if you **agree** with it.

SD····DI····N····(AG)····SA

Mark "SA" if the statement is completely true or if you **strongly agree** with it.

SD····DI····N····AG····(SA)

There are no "right" or "wrong" answers and you don't have to be an expert in order to complete the questionnaire. Describe yourself in a sincere and precise way. Mark your answers in a way that describes you as you are at the present moment and not how you want to be. A failure to answer in an honest way will most likely compromise the test results and yield an unreliable assessment of your personality.

Please answer ALL the questions. Make sure every answer is marked in the enumerated spot in the answer sheet corresponding to its enumerated statement in this booklet.

Questionnaire

1. I do things according to a plan.

2. I make people feel welcome.

3. I want to be the very best.

4. I think that I'm better than other people.

5. I like to solve complex problems.

6. I have frequent mood swings.

7. I try out new things.

8. I do most of the talking.

9. I will agree to anything.

10. I like to plan ahead.

11. I anticipate the needs of others.

12. I want to be in charge.

13. I would like to have more power than other people.

14. I love to read challenging material.

15. I get stressed out easily.

16. I am open to change.

17. I demand attention.

18. I remain calm under pressure.

19. I pay attention to details.

20. I love to help others.

21. I try to surpass others' accomplishments.

22. I boast about my virtues.

23. I can handle a lot of information.

24. I get overwhelmed by emotions.

25. I Let myself go.

26. I speak loudly.

27. I keep a cool head.

28. I demand quality.

29. I feel sympathy for those who are worse off than myself.

30. I try to outdo others.

31. I give in to no one.

32. I carry the conversation to a higher level.

33. I fear for the worst.

34. I prefer variety to routine.

35. I take the initiative.

36. I am calm even in tense situations

37. I set high standards for myself and others.

38. I value cooperation over competition.

39. I never give up.

40. I believe only in myself.

41. I find political discussions interesting.

42. I dislike myself.

43. I like to visit new places.

44. I readily overcome setbacks.

45. I let other people take the credit for my work.

46. I make well-considered decisions.

47. I suffer from others' sorrows.

48. I go straight for the goal.

49. I keep myself well-groomed.

50. I have a rich vocabulary.

51. I get upset easily.

52. I have a vivid imagination.

53. I boss people around.

54. I am not easily bothered by things

55. I detect mistakes.

56. I treat all people equally.

57. I turn plans into actions.

58. I believe that I am important.

59. I enjoy thinking about things.

60. I panic easily.

61. I enjoy hearing new ideas.

62. I like having authority over others.

63. I accept people as they are.

64. I am careful to avoid making mistakes.

65. I sympathize with others' feelings.

66. I plunge into tasks with all my heart.

67. I get upset if others change the way that I have arranged things

68. I formulate ideas clearly.

69. I feel threatened easily.

70. I like to begin new things.

71. I insist that others do things my way.

72. I am on good terms with nearly everyone.

73. I continue until everything is perfect.

74. I am concerned about others.

75. I do more than what's expected of me.

76. I don't care what others think.

77. I am quick to understand things.

78. I take offense easily.

79. I would like to live for a while in a different country.

80. I have a strong need for power.

81. I seldom get mad.

82. I often forget to put things back in their proper place.

83. I tend to dislike soft-hearted people.

84. I carry out my plans.

85. I want to be different from others.

86. I have difficulty understanding abstract ideas.

87. I grumble about things.

88. I seek adventure.

89. I am known as a controlling person.

90. I don't worry about things that have already happened.

91. I take tasks too lightly.

92. I am out for my own personal gain.

93. I get to work at once.

94. I don't care what people think of me.

95. I avoid philosophical discussions.

96. I am very pleased with myself.

97. I can talk others into doing things.

98. I demand to be the center of interest.

99. I yell at people.

100. I leave my work undone.

101. I am not interested in other people's problems.

102. I am not highly motivated to succeed

103. I need the approval of others.

104. I avoid difficult reading material.

105. I feel comfortable with myself.

106. I dislike changes.

107. I am easily discouraged.

108. I snap at people.

109. I am often late to work.

110. I believe people should fend for themselves

111. I do just enough work to get by.

112. I see myself as an average person.

113. I rarely look for a deeper meaning in things.

114. I rarely get irritated.

115. I prefer to stick with things that I know.

116. I have a low opinion of myself.

117. I lose my temper.

118. I am not bothered by disorder

119. I contradict others

120. I put little time and effort into my work

121. I worry about what people think of me

122. I learn things slowly.

123. I am relaxed most of the time.

124. I hate surprises.

125. I am easily intimidated.

126. I won't take the blame for something that's not my
fault.

End of the Test

Make sure you have answered to every statement and proceed to the scoring instructions.

ENNEAGRAM TEST ANSWER SHEET

NAME:					
GENDER:	F M O	AGE:		DATE:	___/___/___

1	SD DI N AG SA	43	SD DI N AG SA	85	SD DI N AG SA
2	SD DI N AG SA	44	SD DI N AG SA	86	SD DI N AG SA
3	SD DI N AG SA	45	SD DI N AG SA	87	SD DI N AG SA
4	SD DI N AG SA	46	SD DI N AG SA	88	SD DI N AG SA
5	SD DI N AG SA	47	SD DI N AG SA	89	SD DI N AG SA
6	SD DI N AG SA	48	SD DI N AG SA	90	SD DI N AG SA
7	SD DI N AG SA	49	SD DI N AG SA	91	SD DI N AG SA
8	SD DI N AG SA	50	SD DI N AG SA	92	SD DI N AG SA
9	SD DI N AG SA	51	SD DI N AG SA	93	SD DI N AG SA
10	SD DI N AG SA	52	SD DI N AG SA	94	SD DI N AG SA
11	SD DI N AG SA	53	SD DI N AG SA	95	SD DI N AG SA
12	SD DI N AG SA	54	SD DI N AG SA	96	SD DI N AG SA
13	SD DI N AG SA	55	SD DI N AG SA	97	SD DI N AG SA
14	SD DI N AG SA	56	SD DI N AG SA	98	SD DI N AG SA
15	SD DI N AG SA	57	SD DI N AG SA	99	SD DI N AG SA
16	SD DI N AG SA	58	SD DI N AG SA	100	SD DI N AG SA
17	SD DI N AG SA	59	SD DI N AG SA	101	SD DI N AG SA
18	SD DI N AG SA	60	SD DI N AG SA	102	SD DI N AG SA
19	SD DI N AG SA	61	SD DI N AG SA	103	SD DI N AG SA
20	SD DI N AG SA	62	SD DI N AG SA	104	SD DI N AG SA
21	SD DI N AG SA	63	SD DI N AG SA	105	SD DI N AG SA
22	SD DI N AG SA	64	SD DI N AG SA	106	SD DI N AG SA
23	SD DI N AG SA	65	SD DI N AG SA	107	SD DI N AG SA
24	SD DI N AG SA	66	SD DI N AG SA	108	SD DI N AG SA
25	SD DI N AG SA	67	SD DI N AG SA	109	SD DI N AG SA
26	SD DI N AG SA	68	SD DI N AG SA	110	SD DI N AG SA
27	SD DI N AG SA	69	SD DI N AG SA	111	SD DI N AG SA
28	SD DI N AG SA	70	SD DI N AG SA	112	SD DI N AG SA
29	SD DI N AG SA	71	SD DI N AG SA	113	SD DI N AG SA
30	SD DI N AG SA	72	SD DI N AG SA	114	SD DI N AG SA
31	SD DI N AG SA	73	SD DI N AG SA	115	SD DI N AG SA
32	SD DI N AG SA	74	SD DI N AG SA	116	SD DI N AG SA
33	SD DI N AG SA	75	SD DI N AG SA	117	SD DI N AG SA
34	SD DI N AG SA	76	SD DI N AG SA	118	SD DI N AG SA
35	SD DI N AG SA	77	SD DI N AG SA	119	SD DI N AG SA
36	SD DI N AG SA	78	SD DI N AG SA	120	SD DI N AG SA
37	SD DI N AG SA	79	SD DI N AG SA	121	SD DI N AG SA
38	SD DI N AG SA	80	SD DI N AG SA	122	SD DI N AG SA
39	SD DI N AG SA	81	SD DI N AG SA	123	SD DI N AG SA
40	SD DI N AG SA	82	SD DI N AG SA	124	SD DI N AG SA
41	SD DI N AG SA	83	SD DI N AG SA	125	SD DI N AG SA
42	SD DI N AG SA	84	SD DI N AG SA	126	SD DI N AG SA

You may photocopy the answer sheet if necessary.

Make sure you have answered to every statement and proceed to the scoring instructions.

SCORING INSTRUCTIONS

Follow these instructions to obtain your scores on the test and diagnose your Enneagram Personality Type. For this, you will need the answer sheet and the scoring sheet.

There are 9 Enneagram personality types. Each personality type has its own score. The score of each personality type is composed of their respective **positively keyed item scores** and **negatively keyed item scores.** Positively keyed item scores are calculated in table 1 of the scoring sheet. Negatively keyed item scores are calculated in table 2 of the scoring sheet. To obtain the score for each personality type, do the following:

Scoring positively keyed items:

Go to table 1 in the scoring sheet. That table contains 9 columns, each one of them represents one of the 9 personality types. Each column is divided into 2 sub-columns: The sub-column on the left contains numbers that represent the item/statement that is going to be scored, this is called an **item sub-column**. The sub-column on the right, which has blank spaces, is where the score for each corresponding item is going to be written, this is called a **score sub-column** (The cells marked with "x" won't be used in this part of the scoring process).

To score an item in the scoring sheet, first, check the answer sheet, and depending on the answer given to the corresponding item, a score will be written in the right sub-column next to the number of the item being scored.

- If the answer to an item is "strongly disagree" (SD), the score of the item will be 1.
- If the answer to an item is "disagree" (DI), the score of the item will be 2.
- If the answer to an item is "neutral" (N), the score of the item will be 3.
- If the answer to an item is "agree" (AG), the score of the item will be 4.
- If the answer to an item is "strongly agree" (SA), the score of the item will be 5.

Example: Scoring item "11"

On the answer sheet: On the scoring sheet:

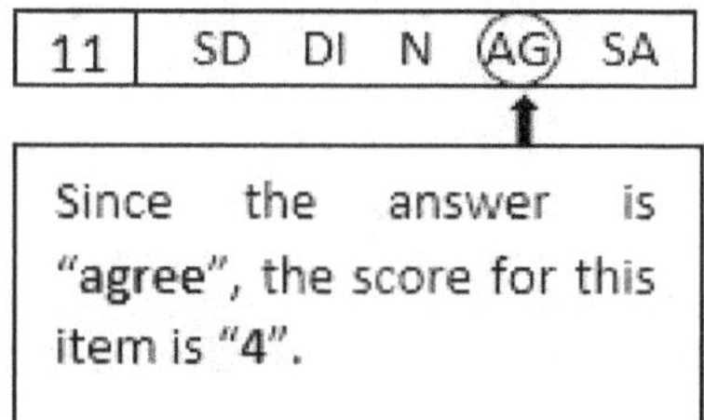

Type 1		Type 2		Type 3	
1		2		3	
10		11	4	12	

Write "4" in the blank space of the score sub-column next to item "11". This item is now scored.

After scoring all the items in the positively keyed items table, proceed to calculate the **positive item score for each type.**

To calculate the **positive item score** for a type, add together all the scores of each **score sub-column** for that type and write the resulting number in the bottom blank space next to the "**P**" labeled cell.

Example: Calculating the positive item score for type 2.

On the Scoring Sheet:

Type 1		Type 2	
1		2	2
10		11	4
19		20	3
28		29	2
37		38	5
46		47	2
55		56	1
64		65	1
73		74	3
x	x	x	x
x	x	x	x
P1		P2	23

Add together all the scores in the **score sub-column** of the Type 2 Column. In this case, the result of the summation is "**23**".

Write the result of the summation in the bottom blank space of the **score sub-column**, next to the "**P2**" cell in the **item sub-column**. The **positive item score for type 2** is now calculated.

After scoring all the 91 items and calculating all the 9 positive item scores in table 1, proceed to calculate the negatively keyed items in table 2.

Scoring negatively keyed items:

Go to table 2 in the scoring sheet. That table contains 9 columns, each one of them represents one of the 9 personality types. Each column is divided into 2 sub-columns: The sub-column on the left contains numbers that represent the item/statement that is going to be scored, this is called an **item sub-column**. The sub-column on the right, which has blank spaces, is where the score for each corresponding item is going to be written, this is called a **score sub-column** (*The cells marked with "x" won't be used in this part of the scoring process*).

To score an item in the scoring sheet, first, check the answer sheet, and depending on the answer given to the corresponding item, a score will be written in the right sub-column next to the number of the item being scored.

- If the answer to an item is "**strongly disagree**" (**SD**), the score of the item will be **5**.
- If the answer to an item is "**disagree**" (**DI**), the score of the item will be **4**.
- If the answer to an item is "**neutral**" (**N**), the score of the item will be **3**.
- If the answer to an item is "**agree**" (**AG**), the score of the item will be **2**.
- If the answer to an item is "**strongly agree**" (**SA**), the score of the item will be **1**.

Example: Scoring item "91"

On the answer sheet:

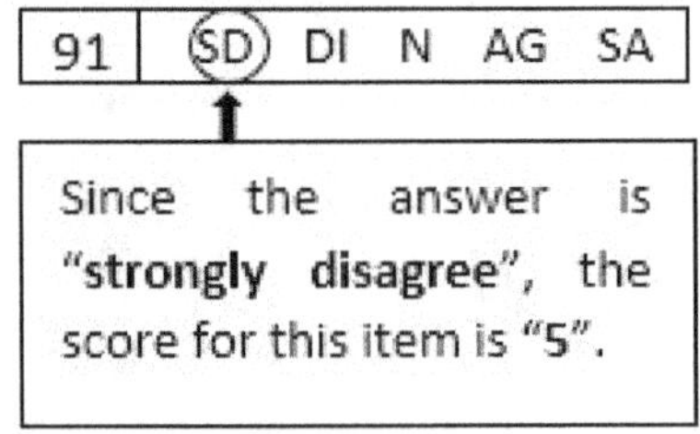

On the scoring sheet:

Type 1		Type 2		Type 3	
82		83		x	x
91	5	92		x	x

Write "5" in the blank space of the score sub-column next to item "91". This item is now scored.

After scoring all the items in the negatively keyed items table, proceed to calculate the **negative item score** for each type.

To calculate the **negative item score** for a type, add together all the scores of each **score sub-column** for that type and write the resulting number in the bottom blank space next to the "**P**" labeled cell.

Example: Calculating the negative item score for type 9.

Type 8		Type 9	
x	x	x	x
x	x	99	4
107		108	2
116		117	5
125		126	3
N8		N9	14

Add together all the scores in the **score sub-column** of the Type 9 Column. In this case, the result of the summation is "**14**".

Write the result of the summation in the bottom blank space of the **score sub-column**, next to the "N9" cell in the **item sub-column**. The **negative item score** for **type 9** is now calculated.

After scoring all the 35 items and calculating all the 9 negative item scores in table 2, proceed to calculate the Total Score for each type.

Calculating the Total Score for each Enneagram Personality Type:

Go to table 3 in the scoring sheet. In here, there are 9 columns, each one of them represents one of the 9 personality types. To calculate the Total Score for each type, add together the **positive item score** and the **negative item scores** for each type and write the resulting number in the bottom blank space of the respective type total score column.

Example: Calculating the Total Score for type 1.

On table 1 (**positive item score**):

On table 2 (**negative item score**):

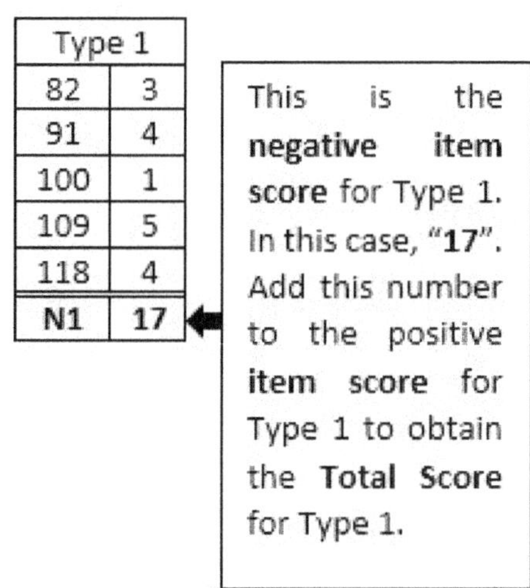

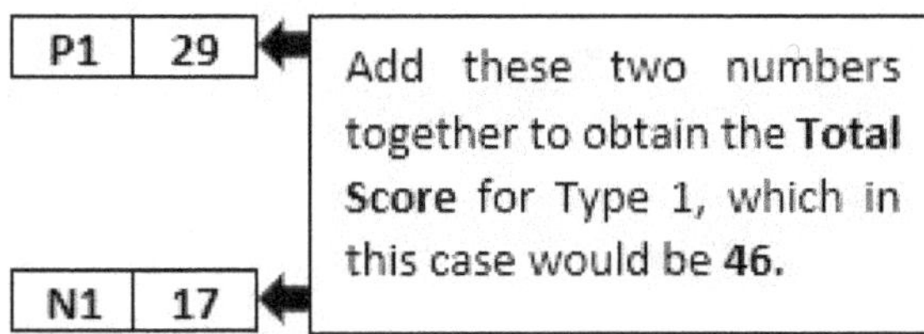

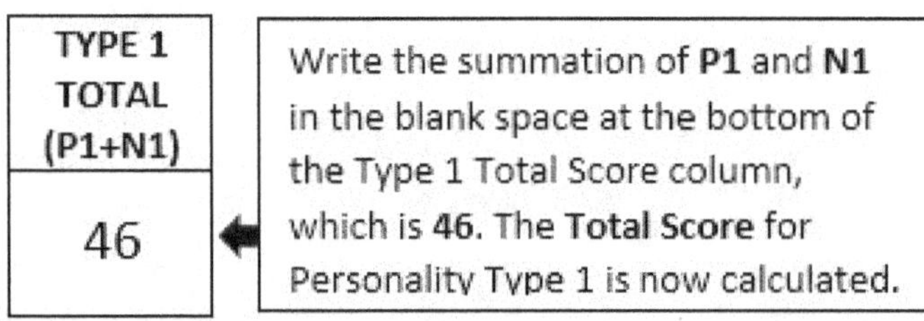

After calculating the Total Scores for all 9 Personality Types, proceed to classify your **most likely, second most likely,** and the **third most likely** personality type.

Classifying most likely personality types:

Go to table 4 in the scoring sheet. In the blank space below the "most likely personality type" cell, write the highest number of the 9 Total Scores for each personality type. In the blank space below the "second most likely personality type" cell, write the second highest number of the 9 Total Scores for each personality type. In the blank space below the "third most likely personality type" cell, write the third highest number among the 9 Total Scores for each personality type.

Example: Classifying most likely personality types:

TYPE 1 TOTAL (P1+N1)	TYPE 2 TOTAL (P2+N2)	TYPE 3 TOTAL (P3+N3)	TYPE 4 TOTAL (P4+N4)	TYPE 5 TOTAL (P5+N5)	TYPE 6 TOTAL (P6+N6)	TYPE 7 TOTAL (P7+N7)	TYPE 8 TOTAL (P8+N8)	TYPE 9 TOTAL (P9+N9)
57	28	41	65	37	54	32	22	50

⬆ Second highest number among the scores.

⬆ Highest number among the scores.

⬆ Third highest number among the scores.

MOST LIKELY PERSONALITY TYPE	SECOND MOST LIKELY PERSONALITY TYPE	THIRD MOST LIKELY PERSONALITY TYPE
4	1	6

In this example, the most likely personality types of the test user are Type 4, followed by Type 1, followed by Type 6.

Note: In this case, there are two or more equal Type Total Scores, they can be considered of equal standing when classifying the most likely personality types. For example, if the highest scores are 56 for Type 3, 52 for Type 7, and 56 for Type 9, the most likely personality type could be classified as Type 3, and the second most likely personality type would be Type 9. The most likely personality type could also be classified as Type 9 with the second most likely being Type 3. In both cases, Type 7 would be the third most likely personality type.

Refer to the **Enneagram Types Overview in Chapter 2** to interpret the test results.

SCORING SHEET

NAME:						
GENDER:	F	M	O	AGE:	DATE:	___/___/___

Table 1: <u>Positively keyed items</u>

Type 1		Type 2		Type 3		Type 4		Type 5		Type 6		Type 7		Type 8		Type 9	
1		2		3		4		5		6		7		8		9	
10		11		12		13		14		15		16		17		18	
19		20		21		22		23		24		25		26		27	
28		29		30		31		32		33		34		35		36	
37		38		39		40		41		42		43		44		45	
46		47		48		49		50		51		52		53		54	
55		56		57		58		59		60		61		62		63	
64		65		66		67		68		69		70		71		72	
73		74		75		76		77		78		79		80		81	
x	x	x	x	84		85		x	x	87		88		89		90	
x	x	x	x	93		94		x	x	x	x	97		98		x	x
P1		**P2**		**P3**		**P4**		**P5**		**P6**		**P7**		**P8**		**P9**	

Table 2: <u>Negatively keyed items</u>

Type 1		Type 2		Type 3		Type 4		Type 5		Type 6		Type 7		Type 8		Type 9	
82		83		x	x	x	x	86		x	x	x	x	x	x	x	x
91		92		x	x	x	x	95		96		x	x	x	x	99	
100		101		102		103		104		105		106		107		108	
109		110		111		112		113		114		115		116		117	
118		119		120		121		122		123		124		125		126	
N1		**N2**		**N3**		**N4**		**N5**		**N6**		**N7**		**N8**		**N9**	

Table 3: <u>Total scores for each personality type</u>

TYPE 1 TOTAL (P1+N1)	TYPE 2 TOTAL (P2+N2)	TYPE 3 TOTAL (P3+N3)	TYPE 4 TOTAL (P4+N4)	TYPE 5 TOTAL (P5+N5)	TYPE 6 TOTAL (P6+N6)	TYPE 7 TOTAL (P7+N7)	TYPE 8 TOTAL (P8+N8)	TYPE 9 TOTAL (P9+N9)

Table 4: <u>Personality types of the test taker</u>

MOST LIKELY PERSONALITY TYPE	SECOND MOST LIKELY PERSONALITY TYPE	THIRD MOST LIKELY PERSONALITY TYPE

Refer to the **Enneagram Types Overview in Chapter 2** to interpret the test results.

Liked What You Read?

I'm always looking for ways to improve! If you enjoyed what you read, then please leave a review on Amazon stating what you liked the most about this book and how it could've been better. **Reviews like yours are the lifeblood of my publishing endeavors. I'm counting with yours!**

Thanks!

Joy Maestri

www.ingramcontent.com/pod-product-compliance
Lightning Source LLC
Chambersburg PA
CBHW082346270726

48658CB00017B/3214